GEOGRAPHY CORNER

Coasts

Ruth Thomson

WAYLAND

Explore the world with **Popcorn -** your complete first non-fiction library.

Look out for more titles in the Popcorn range. All books have the same format of simple text and striking images. Text is carefully matched to the pictures to help readers to identify and understand key vocabulary.
www.waylandbooks.co.uk/popcorn

First published in 2011 by Wayland
Copyright © Wayland 2011

Wayland
Hachette Children's Books
338 Euston Road
London NW1 3BH

Wayland Australia
Level 17/207 Kent Street
Sydney NSW 2000

Produced for Wayland by
White-Thomson Publishing Ltd
www.wtpub.co.uk
+44 (0)843 208 7460

Editor: Steve White-Thomson
Designer: Amy Sparks
Picture researcher: Ruth Thomson/Steve White-Thomson
Series consultant: Kate Ruttle
Design concept: Paul Cherrill

British Library Cataloguing in Publication Data
Thomson, Ruth, 1949-
    Coasts. -- (Geography corner)(Popcorn)
    1. Coasts--Juvenile literature.
    I. Title II. Series
    910.9'146-dc22

ISBN: 978 0 7502 6561 4

Wayland is a division of Hachette Children's Books,
an Hachette UK company.
www.hachette.co.uk

Printed and bound in China

Picture Credits: **Dreamstime**: Camerziga 11, Verastuchelova 13, Tramontana 15, Mangostock 21; **Neil Thomson**: Neil Thomson 23; **Shutterstock**: Robyn Mackenzie (cover), EpicStockMedia 1/7, Juriah Mosin 2/10, Mikhail Zahranichny 4, Patryk Kosmider 5, Kevin Britland 8, Adrian Hughes 9, Carolyn Lamb-Miller 10, Lynsey Allan 10, Ljupco Smokovski 12, Neil Lang 14, sa2324 14 (inset), S. R. Maglione 16, Pichugin Dmitry 17, iofoto s_oleg 19, Vladimir Melnik 20.

Illustration on page 22 by Stefan Chabluk.

Every effort has been made to clear copyright. Should there be any inadvertent omission, please apply to the publisher for rectification.

Contents

What is a coast?

A coast is a place where the sea
meets the land. In some places,
the coast is a sloping beach.

Millions of people visit sandy coasts
in the summer holidays.

In other places, the land
ends with high walls of rock.
These are called cliffs.

The coastline
of a country
is all its land
beside the sea.

High rocky ground that
sticks out into the sea
is called a headland.

 # Waves

Seawater is never still. As wind blows across the sea, it makes waves. Waves slow down as they reach the coast.

Seawater is salty. It is not good for people to drink.

crest

The tops of the waves, called crests, roll over and break onto the shore.

In calm weather, waves are small. In strong winds, waves can be huge. Surfers find it exciting to ride huge waves.

Surfers balance on a surfboard all the way into shore.

 Tides

Twice a day, the sea rises up
the shore and then falls away.
These movements are called tides.

When the tide is high,
the sea covers
beaches and rocks.
It fills harbours
with water.

8

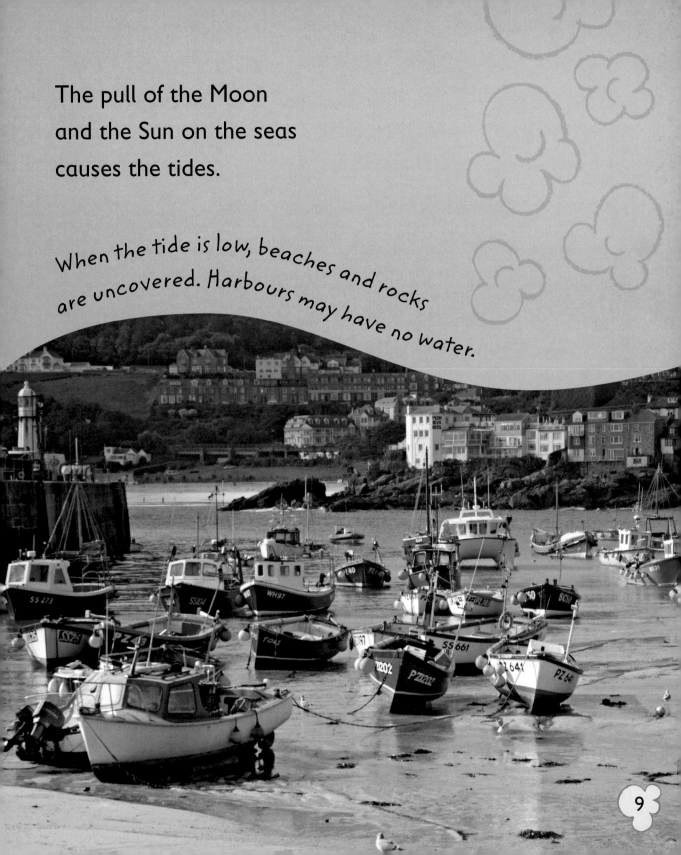

The pull of the Moon
and the Sun on the seas
causes the tides.

When the tide is low, beaches and rocks
are uncovered. Harbours may have no water.

9

Rockpools

Pools of water are left on rocky shores at low tide. These rockpools are home to small fish, shellfish, crabs, sea urchins and starfish.

What can you find in a rockpool?

limpets

sea urchin

Crabs move sideways. They use their powerful claws for cracking shells and fighting other crabs.

Shore crabs are hard to spot because they are the same colour as the rocks.

Rocky cliffs

Wind, rain and waves change
the shape of the coast all the time.
Crashing waves slowly make the
bottom of rocky cliffs crumble.

Waves wear away soft rock, making holes.
These become caves or arches.

Pieces of rock break
off cliffs and smash into
stones on the beach.
Waves roll the stones
against each other.

Stones rub together
and become smooth,
rounded pebbles.

Few plants or
animals can
live on pebbly
beaches.

Sand and dunes

Over millions of years, waves wear soft rocks into tiny grains of sand. Some sandy beaches are made of crushed sea shells.

groyne

close-up of sand

Wooden fences, called groynes, stop waves moving sand along the shore.

Some coasts are always windy.
The wind dries the sand and blows
it behind the beach. The sand piles up
into soft hills called dunes.

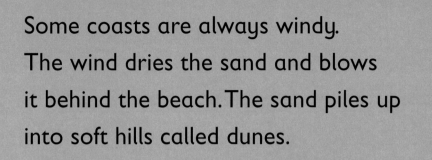

Marram grass is planted on sand dunes.
Its long roots hold the sand in place.

Sea birds and animals

Many sea birds nest and rest together on the ledges of rocky cliffs. Here, they and their eggs are safe from hungry rats, snakes and larger birds.

These puffins dive into the sea to catch prawns and fish. They have webbed feet for swimming.

Seals and turtles are both born on beaches. They swim out to sea soon after they are born.

Seals come back on land to rest. They lie in groups on rocks and sandbanks.

Harbours and ports

Before there were aeroplanes, people travelled across seas by ship. They landed at harbours in deep, sheltered bays. Here, their ships were safe from rough waves.

Sydney, in Australia, has a famous harbour.

Most people in the world live on or near coasts.

Today, ships mainly carry heavy goods. These travel in metal containers. The containers are loaded and unloaded at big ports.

Cranes lift containers off ships straight onto trucks or freight trains.

Protecting coasts

Some people use the sea as a dustbin.
This is dangerous for sea life.
The waste often washes up
onto the shore.

Most waste is plastic. It can float for thousands
of miles before reaching land.

People must look after coasts,
so that these are not spoiled forever.

You can help keep
beaches clean
by picking up
your litter.

A coast at a glance

A coast can have many different features.

beach   bay

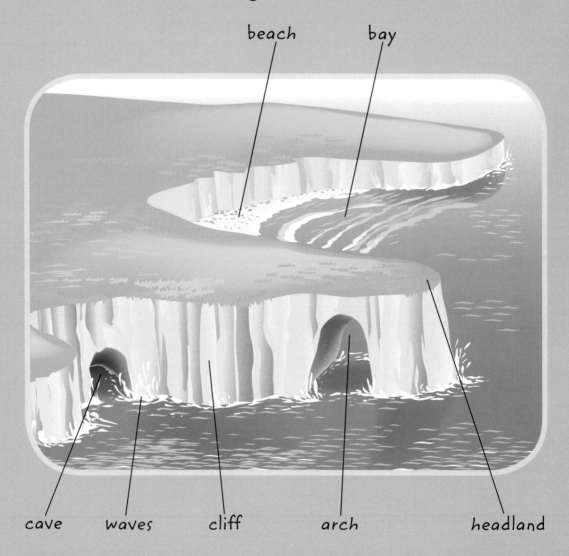

cave   waves   cliff   arch   headland

Draw your own picture of a coast.
Then label it like this picture.

Paint some pebbles

Painted pebbles make good presents for your family or friends.

You will need:
- several pebbles
- paints and paintbrush
- felt-tip pens
- PVA varnish

1. Wash some pebbles and leave them to dry completely.

2. Paint them all over in one colour.

3. When the paint is dry, add details with felt-tip pens to turn each pebble into something funny.

4. Add a coat of clear PVA varnish to make their colours brighter.

Glossary

bay a strip of land on the coast that curves inwards

cave a large hole in the side of a cliff or hill, or underground

freight train a train that carries goods, not people

harbour a place for boats to come in to land, and shelter from rough seas and wind

headland high land that sticks out into the sea

ledge a shelf of rock coming out from the side of a cliff or mountain

port a place where ships load and unload goods

sandbank a hill of sand in the sea

shore the area of land beside the sea

tides the twice-daily rise and fall of the sea

webbed webbed feet have skin joining the toes together

Index

Geography Corner

Contents of titles in the series:

WAYLAND